A GUIDE FOR 21ST CENTURY HIGH SCHOOL STUDENTS

A GUIDE FOR 21ST CENTURY HIGH SCHOOL STUDENTS

JASON ROBERT

To order additional copies of this book, contact:
Xlibris
AU TFN: 1 800 844 927 (Toll Free inside Australia)
AU Local: 0283 108 187 (+61 2 8310 8187 from outside Australia)
www.Xlibris.com.au
Orders@Xlibris.com.au
821656

THE AUTHOR'S PROFILE

Mr. Jason Robert has immersed himself in the teaching profession for the past 18 years. Thus far, he has taught at the University of Science of Malaysia, TAR College(Malaysia), Cambridge Language Centre(Malaysia), Genting INTI International College(Genting Highlands, Malaysia), Limkokwing University (Malaysia, Jakarta and Cambodia), Sunway University, Sunway College, Melbourne Polytechnic(Heidelberg, Melbourne), Topscore Education and Nazareth College in Noble Park, Melbourne, where he is currently attached to as an educator.

He has also spent several years of his career life as a trainer and has conducted staff training on English at Limkokwing University(Malaysia), Goldreign Plastics(Malaysia) and The Royal Police Academy(Malaysia).

Speaking of his academic qualifications, he holds a Bachelor of Business Administration from University Putra Malaysia and a Bachelor of Teaching from the University of Western Sydney. Since migrating to Australia in 2013, he has attained two more qualifications, i.e. the Certificate in Teaching English to Speakers of Other Languages (CELTA) from the University of Cambridge and the Certificate IV in Training and Assessment from Plenty Training, Queensland.

In addition to his unwavering devotion to education, he has proven to be a very versatile educator, considering the multitude of subjects which he has taught thus far, namely a wide array of English subjects, economics, accounting, career & enterprise, statistics, geography, business services, commerce, psychology, business management, music, corporate governance and ethics, mathematics, mathematical methods (advanced mathematics), physics, science, literacy, numeracy, information technology, personal development skills, work-related skills, religion, project management and critical thinking techniques.

Since 2011, he has been involved in professional writing, editing and proofreading. He has written original material for his students, i.e. sample essays and handouts, and was appointed as a writer during his stint at Limkokwing University based on his flair for writing. His writing has been published in *Eternal Portraits*, an American anthology of poems, *GRADUAN 2003*, a magazine for university graduates, *Zenith*, a publication of University Putra Malaysia (UPM) and the Nazareth College newsletter. Furthermore, he has edited Master's and PhD theses and the website content for Mohar Global Services, a Netherlands-based company which promotes international education.

He has been a presenter at international academic conferences, i.e. the International Conference on the Teaching and Learning of Languages (ICTLL 2017), the International Conference on Language Teaching and Learning (IMCICON 2008), the International Conference on Thinking (ICOT 2009) at Kuala Lumpur Convention Centre(KLCC) and the Malaysia International Conference on English Language Teaching (MICELT 2016).

Being a person who engages in lifelong learning and as a person who never rests on his laurels, he always welcomes the idea of delving into new areas or realms of learning.

PREFACE

It is currently the 21st century, a period of time in history where high school students have access to a wealth of information that they require at their fingertips. Despite the convenience of accessing a cornucopia of information on the Internet and/or other sources, there probably has not been a single book that guides exclusively high school students on a multitude of occasions or on various aspects of student life. Personally, I have never come across one. Thus, this book is meant to be a guide for high school students who need instantaneous answers to some or many of their questions, or a guide to those students who may flounder when it comes to public speaking, writing, job interviews, exam preparation, live performances, interpersonal relationships, financial planning, self-organization, and other aspects of high school student life. There might be a sequel to this book in the near future to cover topics omitted in this publication and/or to discuss the content of this book in greater depth. It is hoped that this book shall mitigate the stresses of student life that may be overlooked by society.

Jason Robert

CONTENTS

THE THEORY OF MULTIPLE INTELLIGENCES

Academic excellence is not the only yardstick of success for students. This truth has been illuminated by successful people who did not fare well at school. Take Thomas Alva Edison as a case in point. He became successful in life as a prolific inventor despite being dismissed from school for being too addled to learn. It proves that he was intelligent non-academically.

Having said that, Professor Harvard Gardner, a professor at Harvard University in the United States, has postulated different forms of intelligence that people possess. He has come up with his own theory called "The Theory of Multiple Intelligences", which implies that intelligence is not only manifested in academic grades but also in hands-on experience(knowledge and skills). The theory compartmentalizes intelligence into 9 areas, namely:

1. logical-mathematical intelligence
2. bodily-kinesthetic intelligence
3. naturalist intelligence
4. spatial intelligence
5. musical rhythmic intelligence
6. linguistic intelligence
7. interpersonal intelligence

8. intrapersonal intelligence
9. existential intelligence

Considering the broad scope of this theory, you may delve into it by watching Youtube videos on "The Theory of Multiple Intelligences" or by accessing the website of Adioma under the heading of "9 Types of Intelligence - Inforgraphic", which expounds on the theory.

So, the next time someone tells you that you are not smart or smart enough, you know how to prove them wrong. Focus on at least one forte of yours, out of the nine above, which you can capitalize on to prove how far you can go in life with your self-discovered intelligence. The proof is in the pudding.

STRESS MANAGEMENT

Student life can be exhilarating in many ways; on the flip side, it can be stressful in different ways. Stress emanates from various sources, e.g. uncertainty, fear, the realization of being saddled with a deluge of work with mentally strenuous deadlines, exams, an identity crisis, peer pressure and boredom. Firstly, let's hone in on boredom busters. Below is a list of boredom busters to keep your boredom at bay.

21 Things Which You Can Do When You Are Bored

1. **Look for song lyrics and categorize the lyrics under suitable headings. This could help you to identify the various genres of music.**
2. **Compose songs.**
3. **Write poems about people, life events, abstract concepts, etc.**
4. **Write a story, an article, an essay, etc. for publication.**
5. **Write your life experiences or anecdotes in your personal diary or journal.**
6. **Play indoor games such as chess, checkers, Scrabble, Monopoly, etc.**
7. **Rehearse songs that you would like to render before an audience.**

8. Watch a movie on Netflix, Stan, Amazon Prime or on any other channel.
9. Read a gripping read such as a love novel, an interesting magazine, an anthology, a book on psychology, a biography, etc.
10. Learn something new and/or exciting every day, for example a proverb, a quotation, a word, a Bible verse, an idiom, etc.(Note: According to a book on philosophy, growth is happiness.)
11. Learn new recipes.
12. Listen to some soothing, melodious or endearing music.
13. Acquire new skills such as cross-stitch skills, the skills of painting, the skills of making trinkets, bracelets, necklaces, etc. or the skills of paper art, sand art, web design, interior design, fashion design, etc. The end product could be a wonderful souvenir.
14. Write book/song /movie reviews for publication.
15. Go sightseeing.
16. Chill out with your friends, especially those that you are close to.
17. Snap shots of nature and magnificent/ breathtaking/spectacular sights.
18. Put yourself in a state of reverie to reminisce about the sweet, enchanting past.
19. Log on to Facebook, Instagram, WhatsApp, Snapchat or other social media to check out the photos, especially the evocative ones.
20. Prepare a portfolio that boasts an impressive collection, for example a collection of notes under different themes/genres/headings, etc. or a collection of jokes, idioms, puzzles, party games, ice-breakers, etc.
21. Learn how to play a musical instrument.

Next, let's discuss how you could deal with the stress that comes with exams and homework.

Dealing With the Stress of Exams

When it comes to exams, the more prepared you are, the less stress you are likely to experience. This aligns with the quote below.

If you fail to plan, you are planning to fail.
- Benjamin Franklin

Prolonged hours of studying or revision could be laborious and exhausting, both mentally and physically. Therefore, it is necessary to take short breaks while revising for an exam rather than studying continuously for a prolonged duration of time. It is best to know your own threshold(limit) for a continuous study period before deciding to take a mental break.

If you don't have a mental break, you will have a mental breakdown.
- Jason Robert

Study when you are in the right frame of mind. Studying under sheer exhaustion may not yield the best outcomes. It might not even produce any positive results at all. It is akin to singing. You might not be able to sing as well as you want to when your vocal chords need to rest. Likewise, as suggested by a teacher, you should study based on your mood. Studying when you are not in the right mood can be a sheer waste of time and effort.

Enter the exam hall with confidence, even when you are not fully prepared for the exam. Imagine what could potentially happen to your performance during the exam if your mind is full of negativity, e.g. trepidation, i.e. fear of the unknown(as long as the exam paper has not been leaked), intense fear of failure, lack of confidence, and lack of composure due to pessimism. Negativity could take a heavy toll on your exam performance. You are more likely to pull through an exam by maintaining an optimistic mindset, especially before entering the exam hall. Remember the 3Cs of an exam: clarity of mind(as your mind should be free from unnecessary thoughts), composure or calmness, and confidence.

Dealing With the Stress of Homework

The earlier you start working on your assignments, the less stressed you are likely to be. The journey of doing homework may not always be rosy, exhilarating, or palatable. It could be full of ordeals or 'road bumps'. However, the fruit of learning is always sweet.

The more you talk about the drudgery of homework, the more time is wasted. The key, therefore, is to talk less about your homework agony and do more about eliminating the mounting workload bit by bit and day by day. Time management plays a vital role in achieving your homework goals. In 'SMART' goals, the 'T' refers to 'time bound', so it is imperative to set a deadline or you are only going to procrastinate. 'Later' could mean 'never'.

We will never have time if we only have excuses. - Jason Robert

But bear in mind that time is not the only necessity in completing your tasks. The availability of time is futile if you lack the motivation to complete your assignments. Once again, completing your assignments bit by bit could motivate you to accomplish your tasks. The first step may be the most difficult one but when you are about to 'finish the race', the sense of anticipation could be a source of relief and happiness, a great source of motivation indeed. Imagine being expected to carry a bag of wheat which is extremely heavy. The thought of it itself can put you off easily. However, if you remove the wheat from the bag and put it in 10 different little bags, wouldn't it be manageable as long as you carry one bag at a time? Likewise,

6

that is how you should approach monumental or daunting tasks. In addition, you may put the cart before the horse. You can enjoy yourself as much as you need before you knuckle down to your work, contrary to having the time of your life in celebration upon accomplishing your work. What you choose to do first or later is a matter of preference, but remember to set your priorities right so that your future will be bright.

SELF-MANAGEMENT

To get the ball rolling, it is imperative for you to understand what self-management entails. According to Youth Employment UK(2020), "it means taking responsibility for your own actions and doing things as well as you can." In this section, the focus is on two elements of self-management: self-organization and self-control.

Self-Organization

The best place to plant the seed of self-organisation is your most private space in your home, i.e. your room. If your room is messy, your life is likely to be messy. While this may not be true for each and every individual, there might be a logical explanation to it. Your room is probably your most private space. Having said that, it is most probably the most comfortable space for you to be yourself. If you maintain order in your room, you are likely to maintain order in your school bag, your school locker, your class desk(s), etc. You are also likely to be systematic in the way you organise your possessions when you start working and probably for the rest of your life. Self-organisation can be thought of, metaphorically, as a flower that grows from its seed. Without the seed, the flower does not exist. So, keep your books, notes, and other things in an organised fashion so that your life will not be messy or complicated. Imagine the stress of looking for an item that you have misplaced simply because you have never been organised in the first place. One of the greatest resources that students have is time. The time to be self-organised is now.

Self-Control

Self-control is closely associated with steadfastness. Exercise your wisdom by discerning for yourself what is right and what is wrong. You are responsible for your own actions, and so you need to face the consequences of your actions. Therefore, think rationally when you feel the urge or surge to conform to your friends who befriend vices such as bullying, drugs, alcohol, illegal activities and other vices. Your actions are within your will power; excuses, on the other hand, are a lack of initiative.

An excuse is always a lack of effort.

- Jason Robert

SUCCESS: WHAT IT MEANS & HOW TO ACHIEVE IT

Below is a list of quotes on success to ruminate about.

Success, in its most fundamental sense, is how you feel about yourself. If you feel good about yourself, you are already successful. - Jason Robert

Success is getting what you want. Happiness is wanting what you get. - Benjamin Franklin

In the eyes of a pessimist, failure is a misery, but in the eyes of an optimist, failure leads to glory. Thus, no failure is wasted in the eyes of an optimist. - Jason Robert

Lifelong learning is lifelong adaptation to change. You are successful each time you successfully adapt to change. - Jason Robert

Interest + Determination = Success - Jason Robert

The 4D's of Excellence

Desire → Discipline
→ Determination(Perseverance)
→ Drive(Initiative)

Several Salient Points to Bear in Mind for Success

1. Practise, practise, practise. Practice makes perfect.
2. Have faith in yourself and you shall excel in everything that your heart desires.
3. Have a well-balanced life. It is possible to enjoy life to the fullest and work very hard concurrently.
4. Be optimistic at all times.
5. Don't be discouraged, despondent, or worried when you make mistakes. Every cloud has a silver lining.

QUOTES, WEBSITES & VIDEOS FOR STUDENTS

1. Being ignorant is not so much a shame as being unwilling to learn. – Benjamin Franklin
2. I hear and I forget. I see and I remember. I do and I understand. – Confucius
3. Learn from yesterday, live for today, hope for tomorrow. The important thing is not to stop questioning. – Albert Einstein
4. Live and learn, or you don't live long. – Robert A. Heinlein
5. Enjoy the process of learning and you will enjoy the results. – Jason Robert
6. You have to know a lot to know how little you know. - Author unknown
7. A pessimist sees the difficulty in every opportunity; an optimist sees the opportunity in every difficulty. - Winston Churchill
8. Success is walking from failure to failure with no loss of enthusiasm. - Winston Churchill
9. Practice makes perfect.
10. What is done with pleasure is done to full measure. - Author unknown

11. A good teacher is one who gathers good teaching materials. Likewise, a good student is one who gathers good learning materials. – Jason Robert

If you wish to access more interesting quotes, visit http://www. brainyquote.com.

Useful Websites for Students

1. https://www.simplypsychology.org/
2. http://www.mindtools.com/index.html

Inspirational/Motivational Youtube Videos for Students

1. **Famous Failures (Lesson Available) -BluefishTV.com**
   URL: http://www.youtube.com/watch?v=2dbeJkY6QGk

2. **WHEN LIFE IS HARD - Powerful Motivational Speech**
   URL: https://www.youtube.com/watch?v=RBUuH5fKyyk

3. **Motivational Success Story of Bill Gates - From College Dropout to the Richest Man in the World**
   URL: https://www.youtube.com/watch?v=Q4s_0pNZvnc

SELF-ESTEEM & SELF-LOVE

Self-love is not necessarily an individual's expression of selfishness or self-conceitedness. Nevertheless, when self-love leads to excessive self-narcissism, it can be very unhealthy, not only to the individual but also to others. While some people may perceive self-love as a quality with a negative connotation, it is noteworthy to point out that self-love is actually one of an individual's most essential needs. It is impossible for any individual to be happy in life without self-love. Lack of self-love could also lead to low self-esteem. Unfortunately, nowadays, self-love and self-esteem, for many young adolescents, are closely related to the number of 'likes' that they are given on each social media post. Those social media posters who are depressed due to the depressing numbers of 'likes' must remember that the cyber community who give them the 'likes' that they crave for are potentially people who do not genuinely love them or care about them. Therefore, obsession with the number of 'likes' on a social media post, in that sense, is ludicrous.

You are cool as you are, not because of social media. - Jason Robert

On the other hand, we cannot possibly love others without loving ourselves first. As a case in point, it does not seem sensible to worry about others without taking care of ourselves first. A healthy form of self-love is the one that leads an individual to help others do likewise. Indeed, it is our moral obligation to help other individuals love themselves. In today's digital era, considering the avalanche of social media, it is not uncommon to come across information that is inflammatory, detrimental or false about others. The solution is the Golden Rule: 'Do unto others what you want others to do unto you'. Thus, before we make any comments or respond to any messages about others, for instance on social media, remember the triple filter test of Socrates, which answers the following three questions.

1. Is it true?
2. Is it kind?
3. Is it important?

Time is too precious to waste on criticizing others. Rather, it's better to think of ways in which we can make this world a better place. Don't we want to live in a world of peace, love and harmony? Kindness unto others will eventually or ultimately bear fruit.

THE INFLUENCE OF SOCIAL MEDIA ON SOCIETY

The Netflix documentary entitled "The Social Dilemma" elucidates the detriments of social media comprehensively. The documentary sheds light on the malice of social media companies, whose popular product, i.e. social media, is meant to be addictive to its users so that the companies reap the benefits at the expense of society. Social media is a double-edged product. Nobody can rightfully and honestly debunk the wonderful influence of social media on interpersonal relationships and education. Unfortunately, on the contrary, the negative influence of social media addiction has reared its ugly head in today's society. Social media is insidious. We may not even realise the perils of social media at the moment, but the repercussions may be felt in the long-term, e.g. poor social skills, weak family ties, depression, tragedies, and low self-esteem due to insufficient 'likes'. Social media addiction is as severe as a pandemic, only if we fully understand the extent of damage it has inflicted upon society thus far. The remedy is essentially a personal decision, precisely the decision to have self-control. The quote below aptly relates to the phenomenon of social media addiction at the present moment.

"Sow a thought and you reap an action; sow an act and you reap a habit; sow a habit and you reap a character; sow a character and you reap a destiny." — Ralph Waldo Emerson

Questions to Consider With Regard to Social Media Addiction

1. Which do I value more: my long-term health or the off and on momentary adrenalin rush that comes with social media?
2. What is my priority: the bond of love with my family or my heartless device?
3. Who or what sustains me in difficult times: social media or genuine friends and family members?
4. Which is more valuable: the personal, human touch or the tactile quality of my device?
5. Who or what is my shoulder to cry on: my device or caring people who give me undivided attention?

INTERPERSONAL SKILLS

First and foremost, let's understand what interpersonal skills mean. A UK-based web service company called "Skills You Need"(2020) asserts that "interpersonal skills are the skills we use every day when we communicate and interact with other people, both individually and in groups. They include a wide range of skills, but particularly communication skills such as listening and effective speaking."

The company also maintains that "it is no exaggeration to say that interpersonal skills are the foundation for success in life". If you believe that happiness is a component of success, then it must be pointed out that interpersonal skills are necessary for a good, happy relationship with people, whether they are your family members, relatives, teachers, friends, colleagues, acquaintances, customers or any other category of people.

The greatest happiness in life emanates from relationships.
- Jason Robert

Therefore, while you are still at school, it is advisable to hone your interpersonal skills.

How to Hone Your Interpersonal Skills

1. Be on guard against social media addiction. As implied earlier, social media addiction is highly capable of depriving social media addicts of valuable interpersonal skills, which include conversational skills.

2. Practise your interpersonal skills whenever you have the opportunity to interact with people.

3. Since communication skills are part of interpersonal skills, improve not only your verbal communication but also your non-verbal communication with the assistance of Youtube videos or other digital and non-digital sources.

4. What many students may not realize is the notion that school is a place that gives them the impetus to practise and augment their interpersonal skills. Therefore, be actively involved in class and in extra curricular activities which involve interpersonal interactions.

WRITING E-MAILS

SAMPLE E-MAILS FOR DIFFERENT CONTEXTS

Below are three sample e-mails for three different contexts.

Dear Nicole,

Thank you very much for the email.

With reference to our charity concert report, I am writing to notify you that I am still working on it. I was supposed to knuckle down to it intensively last Friday itself, but due to the commitment of my full-time studies, my progress has been impeded. I hope to complete it by 5 November 2011.

I wish you a pleasant day ahead and look forward to working with you soon.

Regards,

Jack Campbell

Dear Sophia,

Thank you very much for your reply. I apologise for not getting back to you sooner.

I shall submit the requested details once I have obtained them from our clients.

Regards,

Jill Robs

To Whom It May Concern:

This is Jack Fox, a student from Birmingham College who is keen on having some original material published.

Thus far, I have compiled my original quotes and poems which I hope will be published by next year. The material is apt for young adolescents who like to ponder upon life or those who intend to improve the quality of their life.

I am more than delighted to submit the manuscripts to you if you are keen on taking a look at them.

I wish to thank you in advance for your kind attention and anticipate your favourable reply in due course.

Regards,

Jack Fox

Below is a sample e-mail message which can be written for a job application.

Dear Mr Carlton,

I am Lindsy Lee, an experienced mathematics teacher who is keen on applying for the position of mathematics teacher at Luxemborg College.

Please find enclosed a copy of my application letter and curriculum vitae for your perusal.

I wish to thank you in advance for your kind consideration.

Yours sincerely,

Lindsy Lee

Below is a sample e-mail to put forward a proposition.

Dear Mrs Elizabeth,

This is Anne Louise, a teacher from the Women's Institute of Senegal who is keen on collaborating with you in any form of undertaking for the sake of empowering women globally.

For your information, I recently attended your session during the recent Global Women Empowerment Conference, and I feel that I can add value to the work that you do through my talents, e.g. my creativity, versatility, adaptability, flair for writing, and 18 years' experience of social work involving disadvantaged women in several countries in Asia and Africa. The collaboration could be in the form of academic publication, a research project, a conference presentation, or any other form. Armed with unwavering devotion to women empowerment, I am prepared to go the extra mile with the intention of making significant contributions to the well-being of underprivileged women.

I am more than delighted to furnish you with more details on my expertise through my resume or portfolio if you are keen on considering my humble proposition.

Regards,

Anne Louise

Below is a sample e-mail to decline a job offer.

Dear Ms Elena Ross,

Thank you very much for the offer, but I am afraid I have already accepted another job offer.

I wish you all the best in your future endeavours.

Regards,

Jolene Jones

Below is a sample e-mail to invite a prospective participant to a workshop.

Dear Brian,

I would like to invite you to a free workshop entitled "Be Your Own Boss: You Are the Master of Your Life."

The details of the workshop are as follows:

Date: 15 September 2018
Venue: The Sherborne Resort
Time: 10.00 a.m. - 12.00 p.m.

I would appreciate it if you could confirm your attendance at the workshop by 31 August 2018.

Have a pleasant week ahead, and I hope to see you at the workshop.

Yours sincerely,

Pamela Lindsy

Below is a sample response to the e-mail above.

Dear Pamela,

I am writing to confirm my attendance/presence at the workshop.

I wish you a wonderful week ahead and look forward to meeting you at the event.

Yours sincerely,

Brian Lester

SAMPLE ESSAYS

Should Theoretical Examinations Be Abolished?

The question pertaining to the abolition of theoretical exams is one that needs to be delved into with serious, meticulous thought by weighing the pros and cons. Some people may assert that theoretical exams are not necessary and therefore should be abolished whereas some may think that such exams are indispensable for learning. Exams could be useful for learning. Nevertheless, theoretical examinations should be abolished since they impede self-development, promote a passive, unhealthy lifestyle and are stressful.

There is no doubt that theoretical exams are a great source of stress among students. The pressure of performing well in exams emanates from friends, relatives, family members, teachers and peers. It stems from society's tendency to compete with each other and its notion that academic excellence is an indicator or reflection of the quality of students. The stress, in some cases, has been horrendously detrimental in the sense that many students have succumbed to severe depression as a result of failing to cope with the insurmountable stress of exams or their failure to accept the unpalatable reality of obtaining devastating results.

Though theoretical exams impel or motivate students to acquire a great deal of knowledge, they do impede the self-development of students. Students who wish to make the grade in their theoretical exams are obsessed with them to the point that they neglect extra-curricular activities, from which they could derive management skills, leadership skills, communication skills, interpersonal skills, decision-making skills, problem-solving skills, creativity, innovation, etc. Such students fail to realize that company managers or employers are in search of graduates who have such skills, since the value of such skills may surpass the value of excellent academic results.

Theoretical exams, unfortunately, promote an unhealthy lifestyle among students. There are students who are obsessed with passing their exams with flying colours to the point that they neglect an active and a sociable life. They tend to view success in exams too seriously until they do not unwind adequately or savour their leisure sufficiently. They are less interested in social events or get-togethers and sports, which are necessary for the development of a healthy brain. This serves as an impediment to the development of their communication skills, thinking skills and interpersonal skills. Furthermore, theoretical exams promote an excessively sedentary lifestyle, which could be detrimental to students' health.

As it has been elucidated thus far, theoretical exams should be abolished since they have adverse effects on students. More emphasis should be placed on practical examinations, since they are capable of enriching students to a much more impressive degree. It is high time for educational institutions, then, to revamp their assessment structure for the betterment of their students.

MODE: CONTRAST
THESIS: SHOPPING AT THE MINES IS DIFFERENT FROM
SHOPPING AT JAYA JUSCO
AUDIENCE: SHOPHOLICS
METHOD: POINT BY POINT

Being an avid shopper, I revel in patronizing shopping centres, especially shopping malls. I have come to gather that each shopping centre that I patronize offers me a distinctively unique shopping experience due to its uniqueness. For example, shopping at Jaya Jusco is different from shopping at The Mines owing to the fact that there are numerous differences between the two shopping outlets.

Firstly, Jaya Jusco and The Mines differ in terms of architecture. Jaya Jusco, both externally and internally, looks like a simple and conventional supermarket with only two shopping floors. The Mines, on the other hand, is architecturally captivating. The external oriental design of The Mines makes one gaze at it with awe. When a shopper saunters around the interior of the centre, he/she might soak up an enchanting experience of visiting a breathtaking Venice in Malaysia itself. What is more exhilarating is the fact that he/she can cruise along the shopping mall on a ferry. Being a large shopping mall, it has at least 4 shopping floors.

Secondly, The Mines and Jaya Jusco vary in terms of their parking policy. Shoppers who drive to Jaya Jusco are spared from parking charges, since no parking charges are imposed on them if they park their vehicles in the vicinity of the shopping centre. On the contrary, shoppers who drive to The Mines have to pay an exorbitant parking fee of RM6.00 in order to park their vehicles in the premises of the shopping area. The only way they can evade the fee is by parking their vehicles in an area adjacent to the open parking area which is out of the open parking zone.

Perhaps the most outstanding feature that sets a striking line of demarcation between the two shopping centres is the facilities at both locations. Since Jaya Jusco is only an ordinary supermarket by nature, its facilities are limited to ATM machines, fast food restaurants, shopping trolleys, washrooms, etc. apart from the free parking. The Mines boasts an array of facilities that can provide its shoppers or patrons with an enthralling shopping experience and ambience. The facilities include a video arcade, a karaoke lounge, a bowling alley, a pool centre, a cinema, a cruise service, and a multitude of food outlets in addition to the basic facilities such as washrooms, shopping trolleys, ATM machines, etc. It also has a concourse area equipped with a stage, where special events are held occasionally. For instance, it recently organized its "Lantern Festival", which featured a lantern painting contest for children, a mask changing show and a mesmerizing, mind-boggling acrobatic performance by some female acrobats.

In a nutshell, as it has been elucidated thus far, there are apparent differences between Jaya Jusco and The Mines due to their architecture, parking policy, and facilities. This is why the shopping experience at Jaya Jusco is, by far, different from the shopping experience at The Mines. It is difficult to say which shopping outlet is better since it is a matter of absolute subjectivity or individual preference.

Cosmetic Testing on Animals

In the name of progress, we have constantly made strides in various aspects of material life for the sake of our well-being. Unfortunately, we have done so to the point of misusing our role as stewards of creation. As a case in point, animals have been subjected to beauty product testing most inhumanely so that we would be spared from the potential detrimental effects of cosmetics. Indeed, the very fact that animals are mistreated for beauty product testing is egregious for several reasons.

Firstly, animal testing for cosmetic experiments is a heinously inhumane act. An excerpt from the article entitled "Cosmetic Testing on Animals – Inhumane and Unreliable" reads as follows:

> While testing on animals has been used for hundreds
> of years for scientific and medical reasons, only in last

decade or so has it been used for cosmetic purposes. These tests are conducted on a variety of animals, including rats, monkeys, rabbits, kittens, and dogs, and are used to determine whether or not a product is safe for human usage. Two of the more common tests are skin and eye irritation tests, or the Draize test, where the animal (often a rabbit in this case) is put in stocks, has its eyelids "clipped" so that it cannot blink, or has its stomach shaved. Toxic chemicals are then poured or smeared onto its eyes or bare skin and left for days or weeks, being monitored at regular intervals by scientists to see how the toxins affect its skin. No anesthetics are used during this process, meaning that the animal must suffer through the pain until it is killed by the chemicals or put down.

Therefore, these tests prove that human cruelty takes precedence over animal well-being, which is morally unpalatable.

Secondly, cosmetic testing on animals deprives animals of their rights. According to the article "Animals Rights: What are Animal Rights?", "animal interests, however, are not always the same as human interests…However, this should not prevent us from bestowing relevant or appropriate rights on animals." The same article presents the following excerpt:

Relevant rights for animals can be any benefits appropriate for animals that people wish to bestow on them. Relevant rights for animals can include:

The right to live free in the natural state of their choosing.

The right to express normal behaviour (e.g. food searching, grooming, nest building).

The right to life (i.e. not be killed for human food or other human use).

The right to reproduce (i.e. pass on their genes to the next generation).

The right to choose their own lifestyle (e.g. not be coerced into experiments or used as entertainment).

The right to live free from human induced harm (e.g. hunger, thirst, molestation, fear, distress, pain, injury or disease).

Last but not least, vivisection is atrocious since it is a travesty of our role as stewards of creation. Instead of being responsible stewards of creation, we have exercised our superiority to animals by subjugating them to cosmetic testing. In an interview, a PETA (People for the Ethical Treatment of Animals) spokesman said, "Animals differ from humans significantly, making animal drug and cosmetic tests unreliable and dangerous. New research methods, such as computer models, cell cultures and human studies are more accurate, less expensive and much more humane." An excerpt from the article entitled "Animal Tests and Alternatives" reads:

The information that has historically been gained from animal tests is increasingly being replaced with quicker, cheaper and more reliable non-animal methods. Many of the animal tests used to test cosmetics ingredients have now been replaced. These modern methods are more relevant to humans and have been found to predict human reactions better than the traditional outdated animal tests. For example, to assess skin irritation alternatives such as Reconstituted Human Epidermis, like the skin model EPISKIN, can be used. These tests use reconstituted human skin donated from cosmetic surgery and have been shown to be more effective than the original cruel rabbit Draize skin test that they replace. Models also exist and can be used to replace cruel animal tests for eye irritation, the effects of skin sensitization can be predicted by looking at proteins in-vitro (in a test tube), and phototoxicity can also be assessed with a cell based test. When we have discovered alternatives to the excruciating pain and agony inflicted upon animals during cosmetic testing, it is certainly unethical for us, as stewards of creation, to perpetuate cosmetic testing on animals.

As it has been expounded on thus far, the fact that animals are abused for cosmetic product testing is appalling since cosmetic testing is inhumane, deprives animals of their rights and portrays us as poor stewards of creation. Everyone has a role to play in mitigating and eventually eliminating this unhealthy phenomenon from rearing its ugly head in our business-orientated world. It's high time for us to ponder upon the following quote by Mark Twain in ending the outrageous practice of cosmetic testing on animals.

"I am not interested to know whether vivisection produces results that are profitable to the human race or doesn't...The pain which it inflicts upon non-consenting animals is the basis of my enmity toward it, and it is to me sufficient justification of the enmity without looking further." – Mark Twain

Our Relationships With Others Define Who We Are

No man is an island. We therefore cannot exist in isolation throughout our lives. Abraham Maslow, in his hierarchy of needs, postulates that society needs to have a sense of belonging, i.e. we have an inherent need to interact with others. Our relationships with others, e.g. our family, our friends and the communities that we come in contact with, play an integral role in our lives as they shape and mould us into who we are. In other words, our relationships with others define who we are.

First and foremost, let us consider how our relationship with our family defines us. Parents, either consciously or subconsciously, play the noble role of teaching their children lessons of life. They inculcate the values that they believe in in the hearts and minds of their children, who may hold on to those values steadfastly throughout their lives. As a case in point, children who are brought up in strict, religious upbringing are likely to grow up in appreciation of their faith and lead their life based on the tenets of their faith such as abstinence from drug addiction, alcoholism, and any other egregious vice.

In addition, many children follow in the footsteps of their parents in terms of their professional life. Katie Hudson, for instance, has pursued a career in acting as her mother, Goldie Hawn, was an actress. Julian Lennon immersed himself in music just like his father, John Lennon. Likewise, it is likely for a child to be a lawyer if their father/mother is a lawyer. It is likely for a child to be in the world of business if their father/mother is in business. It is likely for a child to be a politician if their father/mother is a politician.

We are also influenced by our siblings in various ways. Based on Albert Bandura's theory of social learning, we may copy the behaviour of our siblings by pursuing similar interests and embracing similar lifestyles and values. The Osmonds, The Jackson Five, The Bee Gees, The Everly Brothers and The Corrs are just a few examples of how siblings could define each other in terms of career life.

Our relationship with our friends also defines who we are. There is a saying that goes: Tell me who your friends are and I'll tell you who you are. It is worth reiterating that we replicate the behaviour of others as suggested by Albert Bandura through his social learning theory. This includes the clothes that we wear, the lifestyles that we embrace, the values that we live by, and so on. At the same time, in order to maintain or strengthen friendship, there is pressure to conform to the expectations of our peers. Peer pressure could exert great influence over us, which is the reason why our friends are capable of defining us. For instance, if our friends indulge themselves in smoking, drinking, unhealthy partying, drugs, and other vices, we are likely to conform to their life and be like them. Therefore, they define us in terms of our values, lifestyles and personality. On the other hand, if our friends are into religious events, spiritual health or well-being, reading, self-development, travelling, and other healthy recreations, we are likely to follow in their footsteps. In the long-run, we may share mutual values, lifestyles and eventually become a person of good conduct and character.

Last but not least, our relationships with the communities that we come in contact with define us. The communities that we come in contact with may include our colleagues, i.e. our community at work, the members of a club/society/professional association that we belong to, members of a church or any other religious group, etc. As a case in point, excellent and caring managers at work motivate us and lead us to professional success through their faith in us, their wisdom, experience, charisma and commendable leadership. As a result, we emulate their good qualities and develop ourselves, either consciously or subconsciously, in terms of leadership, time management, self-motivation, self-discipline, communication skills, interpersonal skills, problem-solving, tenacity and other qualities. On the contrary, managers who are condescending and ruthless may turn us into a bitter person who is full of resentment, negativity, low self-esteem, and low self-motivation. Likewise, our colleagues, through their interactions with us, precisely through the manner in which they treat us, determine what kind of person we become eventually. When they are optimistic and lively, they are likely to radiate their optimism and liveliness unto us, prompting us to be optimistic and lively like them, and vice versa. The same is true when it comes to our religious community. Our religious leaders who lead by example teach us to do likewise in living our religious principles in our day-to-day life and we become a role model to others. They inspire us and mould us to be a better person and live a healthy and God-centred life rather than a merely worldly, hedonistic life with no guiding principles or ethics. The leaders and members of a society, club or association that we belong to have the same influence upon us. They can bring out the best in us through their inspiring life or demeanour, wisdom, advice, encouragement and support. We, in turn, emulate them and develop ourselves of our own accord.

As it has been elucidated thus far, our relationships with others, e.g. our relationships with our family, friends and communities, define us, i.e. they make us who we are. It implies that such relationships bring out our negative and positive qualities; thus, they bring out the best and worst in us. It is therefore necessary for us to establish healthy relationships with the people that we come in contact with, either in person or digitally via social media and/or other means, in the hope that the relationships enable us to grow and make strides in life in various ways, e.g. personally, physically, professionally, emotionally and spiritually.

A SAMPLE SCHOOL
MAGAZINE ARTICLE

The Graduation Day of Champion College on 24 July 2010

Tumultuous shouts of triumphant joy and jubilation reverberated across the Hall of Fame of Champion College on 24 July 2008 as it was a momentous day for the 656 graduates of the college, who received their much coveted awards. Considering the overwhelming number of graduates, for the first time in the history of the college, there were 2 graduation sessions - one in the morning and the other in the afternoon.

The founder and president of the college, Dr Hutton White, expressed his earnest gratitude to the parents of the graduates, who had raised their children with painstaking care, love and devotion. In addition, he challenged the graduates to be the best in whatever that they were to embark on, and encouraged them to strive towards seeing their dreams come to fruition by citing real-life exemplary models of success, namely the founders of Facebook, Myspace, and Twitter. The event was augmented by endearing song renditions by the college choir and solo singers, who belted out famous hits such as "You Raise Me Up" with the accompaniment of the choir, "Don't Stop Believing", "I'm Alive" and "You're Simply The Best".

Aliyah, the graduate from Bosnia Hezergovinia who delivered her valedictorian speech, said that Champion College is indeed a remarkable melting pot as she could think of no other place in the globe that boasts such an eclectically rich cultural composition. She also pointed out that the concept of learning at the college transcends books. Saif, the Tanzanian graduate who delivered his speech, impressed the audience with his fluent Indonesian, and debunked the delusion that true friends are hard to find in a foreign land. The Bostwanan graduate who delivered his speech in the afternoon session was emotional when he recalled his dear friend who could not graduate with him on the auspiciously memorable day due to unforeseen circumstances. Prior to his address, the words of the Malaysian graduate from the Department of Media, Communication & Broadcasting during her presentation must have struck a chord with the audience as they were amazingly inspirational. She spoke of the ebb and flow of her college life, i.e. her odyssey of conquering victory after all the harsh realities that she had had to come to terms with as a result of her obesity.

After the afternoon ceremony, the graduates and parents proceeded to the Sheraton Plaza, where they were treated to the buffet meal and live entertainment by the Sound & Music Academy. Some of the staff filled the atmosphere with exhilaration when they danced delightfully on their self-declared dance floor. A few of the graduates from the Sound & Music Academy couldn't repress their intense impulse to flaunt their musical prowess. Through their knack for music, they successfully mesmerized their audience, who listened to their music with rapture.

All in all, it was certainly a day for the delirious graduates, parents and the college staff to cherish, treasure and fondly remember.

A SAMPLE MEMORANDUM

MEMORANDUM

From : Jones Black
To : Ms Izzy Fernandez
Date : 19 January 2009
Subject: Annual Leave

With reference to the matter above, allow me to bring to your attention that I still have 10 days of annual leave from 2008 and 2009, which I need to use up by the end of March 2010.

For practical reasons, I wish to have the time period for the clearance of my annual leave extended to the end of 2010.

I earnestly hope that you will accede to my supplication. I would like to thank you in advance for your kind consideration.

WRITING ADVERTISEMENTS ON A COMMERCIAL WEBSITE

Here is a template for an unsolicited job application for a commercial website such as Gumtree.

Good day! I am _____ and I have just completed my Certificate in_____, which included my apprenticeship at _____. The 3-month stint has equipped me with skills in _____. I am industrious, disciplined, reliable and conscientious. Since I am always eager to learn, I never rest on my laurels. I am available for work from Monday to Friday. Please do not hesitate to contact me if you have any queries. I could be reached on _____ or via e-mail at _____.

Be proactive in your job search. Unsolicited job applications could potentially earn you your dream job.

- Jason Robert

A SAMPLE JOB APPLICATION LETTER

10 October 2020

Joe White
2/18 Fortitude Ct
Sir Browning Park, QLD 3803

Ms Cherry Lindberg
Principal
Methodist Girls' School
141 Heaven Highway
Manson Park, QLD 3987

Dear Ms Lindberg,

APPLICATION FOR THE POSITION OF MATHEMATICS TEACHER

Referring to the matter above, I would like to apply for the position of mathematics teacher at Methodist Girls' School due to my unbridled passion for assisting students to attain numerical and reasoning proficiency.

For your information, I have been at the service of St Theresa's College since January 2019 as a teacher and teacher aide. Thus far, I have devotedly rendered my service at the school by teaching and rendering learning support or assistance to students with learning needs, especially in mathematics. My teaching stint at Intelligent Polytechnic as a VCAL teacher paved the way for teaching a broad range of subjects up to the senior level, including numeracy and critical thinking techniques. In addition, I have worked for Broadminded Education as a mathematics tutor since March 2014. Under the highly reputable tutoring company, I have taught mathematics to predominantly high school students of various levels.

As a fervent educator, nothing delights me more than the difference that my tutelage brings to my students, both academically and personally. I take great pride in the fact that my former Year 6 student emerged as the dux of Lynsy Primary School in 2015.

Besides being disciplined and meticulous, I ardently believe in performing my duties expeditiously and regard quality very highly. Please find enclosed a copy of my curriculum vitae, which gives more details on my personal traits, for your perusal.

I shall be more than delighted to fix an appointment with you at your convenience. I would like to thank you in advance for your kind consideration and eagerly anticipate your favourable reply in due course.

Yours sincerely,

Joe White

A SAMPLE CURRICULUM VITAE

JOE WHITE

2/18 Fortitude Ct, Sir Browning Park, QLD 3803, Australia
Email: cool_joe@yahoo.com
Mobile: +6176890434

PERSONAL TRAITS

- Possess good interpersonal, leadership, and communication skills
- Responsible, able to manage and motivate a team, and highly reliable
- Helpful, generous, industrious, conscientious and meticulous

OTHER SKILLS

- IT skills: PowerPoint(including animation), Microsoft Excel, Zoom, GoogleMeet, social media; data encryption, website content creation;
- event planning and coordination
- emceeing
- networking

EDUCATION

September 2014   Certificate IV in Training & Assessment
Crown Training Institute
Queensland, Australia

EMPLOYMENT HISTORY

Jan 2019 – Present   Teacher/Teacher Aide/Homework Club Tutor
St Theresa's College(Fortitude Valley, Queensland)
Responsibilities: Teaching, exam supervision, assessment, rendering learning support/assistance to students with learning needs, helping out at school events

PROFESSIONAL & PERSONAL DEVELOPMENT

21 April 2019	Business presentation: Effective Communication for Better Results (Presenter – Celebrity Bank)
3 – 4 April 2017	International Conference on the Teaching and Learning of Mathematics (Presenter – The Royal Hotel)
22 – 26 June 2009	International Conference on STEM (Presenter – GoGreen Convention Centre, Geneva)
June 2004	STEM Skills Forum 2001 (Volunteer - Pitty Python Park, Thailand)

EXTRA-CURRICULAR ACTIVITIES & ACHIEVEMENTS

Leadership

2001	Vice-President of the Business Club (Blue Ocean University)
2000	President of the English Literary Society (Blue Ocean University)

Entertainment

2012   Staged a song performance at several events of Capernaum College, i.e.

* ❖ "Australian Matriculation(AUSMAT) Awards Night 2012"
* ❖ "Intensive English Programme Department Chinese New Year cum End-of-Semester /Farewell Party"
* ❖ "Australian Matriculation(AUSMAT) Teachers' Day"
* ❖ "Busking for Charity Festival"

Others

22 July 2017   Volunteered as a course marshal at "Stadium Stomp" (a charity event to raise funds for The Leukaemia Foundation) Venue: Melbourne Cricket Ground, Melbourne

6 Nov 2017   Volunteered as a pin seller during the Melbourne Cup season to raise funds for JDRF (a charity which funds type 1 diabetes research) Venue: Flemington Racecourse, Melbourne

REFEREES

Name	:	Mr Sulky Hutton
Position	:	Director of Broadminded Education
Location	:	Suite 98, 76 Ellis Parade, QLD 3903
Telephone	:	03879076532
E-mail	:	shutton@broadmindedducation.com.au

Name	:	Mr Giddy Hulk
Position	:	Director of Proton Polytechnic
Location	:	Suite 143, 76 Chrysler Avenue, QLD 3785
Telephone	:	0387965322
E-mail	:	hulkgiddy@protonpolytechnic.com.au

SAMPLE SPEECHES FOR DIFFERENT CONTEXTS

A very good evening to all those who are present here tonight, especially the guests of honour and the parents. Welcome to "Samba Night".

As the General Manager of "Samba Night", I would like to firstly express my gratitude to all my teammates for the determination and hard work that they have displayed for the success of tonight's event. I truly appreciate their highly commendable effort. I would also like to thank Mr. Lousy Frosty, Mr. Kennedy, Chef Redhead, Chef Ricardo, Mr. Rich and Mr. Ryan for the support and guidance that they have rendered to me. Allow me to specially thank all the sponsors who have been remarkably supportive of tonight's event. They include Coffee Terrain, The Palmolive, the Cool Breeze Hotel, Spring Convention Centre, the Black Hole Restaurant and Cocoa Powder. The last group of people that I would like to thank is the guests, for without the presence of the guests, I believe, the event wouldn't be an exhilarating one.

Last but not least, I hope that all of you will savour the night to the fullest. May the memories of the event be indelibly imprinted on your minds.

Thank you for your kind attention, and enjoy the night.

Greetings of joy to all those gathered at this stupendous Hall of Fame. I indeed feel privileged and fortunate to have been selected to deliver my speech at this significant event. Under the tutelage of enthusiastic, approachable and diligent lectures, I have been able to widen my horizons in various fields.

All the sweet memories and moments that have adorned my life at this college will be indelibly imprinted on my mind. Those phenomenally sensational moments can never possibly efface from my memory.

I personally must attest to the fact that Victory College has progressed by leaps and bounds since I initiated my life as a student here.

Now, I am prepared to savour a journey of exciting challenges that await me in the realm that I am most passionate about, which is none other than the field of advertising itself.

I would like to earnestly thank all those who have made my life here a truly eventful, meaningful and memorable one. Thank you for your kind attention, and enjoy the rest of the day.

Below is a sample speech for a donation appeal drive.

Good evening, dear friends.

My name is Stuart Johnson and I am a member of the college's St Vincent de Paul Society.

As you can see in the school newsletter, we have shed light on how profoundly your unremitting support to us has borne fruit for the less fortunate in our community. Our gratitude to your love, manifested through your unconditional generosity, defies description.

Your continuous support has helped us to champion so many worthy causes for so many who are constantly in need of your benevolence. I believe that you will be blessed bounteously for your compassionate generosity.

On behalf of the St Vincent de Paul Society, I sincerely thank you for your kind and rapt attention, unwavering support and commendable kindness.

Thank you, friends. May God bless all of you.

A Sample Speech for a Charity Run Event

A very good morning to all the distinguished guests of honour, the organisers of "Run4Harmony", and all the participants of this noble event. It is indeed a great privilege, honour and pleasure for me to be in attendance at an event like this, which champions a worthy cause.

As you may already be aware of, "Run4Harmony" is an annual event which takes places in all corners of the world within the same week. I am proud of the fact that for the very first time, it takes place in Malaysia. What excites me even more is the fact that it takes place in this historically and culturally magnificent state of Penang.

We must all be clear about the purpose or objective of "Run4Harmony", which is to foster unity and peace among young adolescents of multiple ethnic groups, cultures and religions. The whole world today is in need of peace and unity, especially among today's young adolescents, who will be the leaders of tomorrow.

The objective of "Run4Harmony" could only be achieved through the Golden Rule, which postulates that we must do unto others what we want others to do unto us. The Golden Rule is a tenet which I believe is propagated in every religion of the world. The Golden Rule enables us to put aside our differences and focus on the similarities that we share, especially the fact that we are people who have the need for a sense of belonging. It is through events like this that such a simple but profoundly meaningful message of the Golden Rule, which is key to global peace and unity, could resonate throughout the world.

I would like to take this opportunity to express my gratitude to the organisers of this event, namely the Church of St. Anne and the Focolare movement, for working unwaveringly and steadfastly for the success of this event, which will benefit everyone here.

I hope that all of you here will make the most of this momentous event and have a wonderfully memorable day ahead.

Thank you for your rapt attention, and may God bless you.

A Sample Farewell Speech

Good evening, dear friends. They say that every good thing must come to an end. Today, with a heavy heart, I have to bid farewell to all of you, who are so significant to me, for who you truly are and what you have done for me. Words alone are not sufficient to express my gratitude to all of you. As I embark on my career in a new city, I hope that this is not the end of our strong ties. I shall miss you dearly, and you will always be in my heart. Remember FRANCE, which is the acronym for 'Friendship Remains And Never Can End'. I wish you all the best in your undertakings and hope to be reunited with you in the future. Please feel free to visit me in my new place, and I shall be more than delighted to welcome you with open arms. Thank you once again and goodbye.

A Sample Birthday Speech

Good evening, dear friends. I am going to keep my speech short and sweet. First and foremost, I thank each and every one of you from the bottom of my heart for your invaluable presence at my birthday party, which means so much more than the presents which you have given me. I hope you have had a ball tonight. It has been an amazing and special night for me thus far, and I hope you will continue to have much more fun. We were born to have fun, so party on!!!!!

JOB INTERVIEWS

Attending a face-to-face job interview can be a nerve-wracking experience for some students; however, with adequate preparation, you may feel less anxious. Approach a job interview the same way you approach an exam. Therefore, the same recommendations for exam preparation discussed previously may work well for job interviews. They say that the first impression is the last impression, so you ought to take each interview seriously. It is necessary to exude confidence and calmness during a job interview; thus, meticulous preparation for a job interview could be a factor of success at an interview. There is no guarantee that you will secure a job after being successful at a job interview. However, every interview that you attend will be able to arm you with the knowledge or experience to make strides in your future job interviews; so, no interview is a waste of time and effort if you see the big picture of job interviews. At a job interview, endeavour to create the impression that you will be an asset to the interviewer(s) through your amiable personality, sense of humour, skills, academic qualifications and working experience. One question that you can anticipate at a job interview is : Tell me about yourself. As a guide, you can cover the following points to answer the question.

1. Your academic qualification(s)
2. Your working experience, including your experience of volunteering at various events and places

3. Your personal skills such as IT skills, communication skills and problem-solving skills
4. Your personal attributes, e.g. your discipline, sense of focus and tenacity
5. Your interests(Note: Do not mention interests such as partying and gaming, even if they are true, as the interviewer(s) may not have a good opinion of you.)

Be courteous at all times, even if you disagree with the interviewer(s). At the same time, be humble and give the company the impression that you are willing to learn, and that you thrive on challenges. In the event where the wages are not fixed, or are not standard rates, give a reasonable range for your wages.

To be a good communicator, use words effectively. To be a great communicator, use words and non-verbal communication effectively.

- Jason Robert

FINANCIAL PLANNING

Making a Living While You Are at School

Wise students utilise their time productively to their advantage. They realise that time is too precious to waste on unnecessary or futile self-indulgence. They may not be obsessed with activities such as gossiping about their peers, being too nosey about celebrities' private lives, posting hate messages on social media, and extravagant online shopping. Such students capitalise on their time, an invaluable resource at their disposal, and their talents with a goal in mind, which could be: to develop themselves, to prepare for their future, or to make a living while studying. There are plenty of ideas that you can think of to make a living while still studying: blogging, creating content for Youtube, working at a supermarket or fast-food chain, starting an online business, recycling for cash and the list goes on. The sky is the limit.

Time + Talents = Treasures - Jason Robert

Spending vs Saving: Which Should I Prioritise?

It's not surprising that young adolescents have the impulse to spend money since many of them have free access to cash. After all, life is to be enjoyed to the fullest, and as suggested by One Direction in "Live

While We're Young", we should "live while we're young". However, remember that rash spending may lead to an extravagant lifestyle in a competitive society, potentially bringing about the insecurity of not being able to live up to the "ideal life" of students who belong to affluent families; these wealthy students' lives may be full of glitz and glamour as the saying goes: Not all that glitters is gold. The solution is simple and the answer is simply simplicity. Perhaps as a good rule of thumb, you can spend 40% of the money that you receive from your parents or other means and save or invest 60% of the money for future ventures. The three quotes below are worth pondering upon when you feel tempted to spend impetuously.

When we have what we need, we don't need what we want. - Jason Robert

Contentment is natural wealth; luxury is artificial poverty. - Socrates

Save money for a rainy day.

SERVICE TO HUMANITY

"Intelligence plus character. That is the goal of true education."
                                        - Martin Luther King

Education is futile if it does not positively impact the character or virtues of students. Based on this assertion, education and good character are inextricable.

In addition, education is not only about attaining stellar academic grades. Education is not only about having a stupendously lucrative career. Education, in a holistic sense, transcends academic qualifications and successful career positions. Education includes service to humanity. If service to humanity is not a strand or tentacle of education, then true education does not exist in its holistic sense. Education is about inspiring others to reach great heights. Education is about bringing out the best in others. Education is about making a difference to the world with whatever that we have and whosoever that we reach out to. Take some time to reflect upon the pearls of wisdom below, which are related to service to humanity.

When you are on fire, others you inspire.
                                        - Jason Robert

You have to be on fire to inspire others and not retire.

-Jason Robert

One of the greatest joys in life is the joy of bringing joy to others.

-Jason Robert

It is a privilege to sleep every night with a clear conscience and peace of mind. It's a privilege that is often taken for granted.

-Jason Robert

It's not about the money. It's about the legacy. The legacy is worth more than the money.

-Jason Robert

HUMOUR: ITS POWER ON STUDENTS' LIFE

We may be attuned to the proverb that goes: Laughter is the best medicine. Apart from making the most of humour to increase your happiness, you can take advantage of humour to augment your interpersonal communication. According to the article entitled "Building Rapport With Humour", "humour is one of the most powerful tools we have in our arsenal of communication, because it is the easiest and most effective way to build a rapport with someone"(Stacey, 2012). Therefore, you can use humour to enhance your interpersonal skills with different categories of people, including those that you meet for the first time, be it at a birthday party, a school event, an inter-school competition, or on any other social occasion.

In addition, you can take advantage of humour to aid or facilitate your learning. According to Itamar Shatz, a PhD student of Cambridge University, "one of the main benefits of humor is that people are generally better able to remember information that they perceive as humorous, compared to information that they don't perceive as humorous." He asserts that "when students are taught a new concept in a humorous way, such as through a funny story, they're generally more likely to remember that concept, compared to if it was taught in a non-humorous manner."

So, the next time you meet a boring teacher or tolerate a boring class, do something about it using your creativity. While you may be inclined to blame the teacher or the class, perhaps you can unleash your latent creativity to bring out the humour buried within you. Learning can be exhilarating when you know how to learn creatively, especially by infusing humour into learning. Therefore, strive to turn a bad situation to a positive experience through humour.

> **BAD is an acronym for "boring", "annoying"**
> **and "depressing".**
>
> **- Jason Robert**

Below is an example of how creativity can make learning humorous and compelling. You could add a line to a quote which already exists. Take a look at the quote below as an example.

Strike while the iron is hot. **When it's cold, you'll be too old**. - Jason Robert

This new line added to the original quote could possibly help a student remember the proverb better, especially when it is used to encourage a guy or girl not to delay in confessing their feelings to those that they fancy before someone else "cuts their grass". (Note: According to the Urban Dictionary, cutting someone's grass happens "when a person, whether they're your friend or not, tunes or tries to chat up the person you're trying to tune or chat up and steal them from you.")

The next example below can be used to tease a close friend so that they will be focused on learning rather than whiling away their time or mucking about.

All work and no play makes Jack a dull boy. **All play and no work makes Jack a dumb boy.** - Jason Robert

Once again, it is easier for a student to remember the original proverb when there is a tinge of humour added to it.

The third example below shows how academic jargon or concepts can be illustrated through scintillating analogies. The author of the riveting article below is still unknown. Nevertheless, for leaving behind a wonderful legacy, what is known is the author's amazing creativity.

10 Amusing Marketing Concepts

1. **Direct Marketing** **You see a gorgeous girl at a party. You go up to her and say: "I am very rich. Marry me!"**
2. **Advertising You're at a party with a bunch of friends and see a gorgeous girl. One of your friends goes up to her and pointing at you says: "He's very rich. Marry him."**
3. **Telemarketing You see a gorgeous girl at a party. You go up to her and get her telephone number. The next day, you call and say: "Hi, I'm very rich. Marry me."**
4. **You're at a party and see a gorgeous girl. You get up and straighten your tie, you walk up to her and pour her a drink, you open the door (of the car)for her, pick up her bag after she drops it, offer her ride and then say: "By the way, I'm rich. Will you marry me?" – That's Public Relations.**
5. **You're at a party and see a gorgeous girl. She walks up to you and says: "You are very rich! Can you marry me?" – That's Brand Recognition.**

6. **You see a gorgeous girl at a party. You go up to her and say: "I am very rich. Marry me!" She gives you a nice hard slap on your face.** – <u>That's Customer Feedback.</u>
7. **You see a gorgeous girl at a party. You go up to her and say: "I am very rich. Marry me!" And she introduces you to her husband.** – <u>That's Demand and Supply Gap.</u>
8. **You see a gorgeous girl at a party. You walk up to her and before you can say anything, another person comes along and tells her, "I am very rich. Marry me!" That's MARKET COMPETITION.**
9. **You see a gorgeous girl at a party. You walk up to her and before you can say anything, another person comes along and tells her, "I am very rich. Marry me!" And she follows him. That's LOSING MARKET SHARE.**
10. **You see a gorgeous girl at a party. You walk up to her and before you can say, "I am very rich. Marry me!", YOUR WIFE TURNS UP! That's BARRIER TO NEW MARKET ENTRY.**

Source: https://virtual-kidspace.blogspot.com/2013/06/10-amusing-marketing-concepts.html

ROMANTIC RELATIONSHIPS

Below are some tips for guys who are interested in going after girls based on personal experience and/or personal opinions.

Tips for Guys Who Want to Go After Girls

1. Show girls that you genuinely like/love them.
2. Girls are sentimental, so you must touch or mend their hearts.
3. Girls are interested in what guys can provide them with(e.g. security, comfort, appreciation, and companionship).
4. Be yourself so that you would be comfortable with them. Thus, do not pretend to be what you are not before them.
5. Be honest with them.
6. Compliment them, but do not overdo it.
7. Smile at them, but do not overdo it.
8. Be a gentleman at all times. Buy them gifts, and take them to dinners and lunches at your expense.
9. Girls like guys with a good sense of humour.
10. Ask them a lot of questions, but do not ask them too many questions in one go.
11. Think of topics to talk about, which include movies, current issues which are derived from social media, the news, etc. to prolong conversations.
12. Once in a while, tell them that you like them.

13. Do not portray the image that you are a creepy predator.

Below are some interesting tips for girls who want to win the hearts of guys.

Tips for Girls Who Want to Impress Guys

1. Show them your affection by caressing them.
2. Give them heavenly surprises.
3. Buy them gifts that they value (e.g. computer games, high-tech tools, Blu-ray discs, CDs, etc.).
4. Cook for them, and with them.
5. Compliment them once in a while.
6. Make them proud of you so that they can brag about you when they are in the company of their male friends.
7. Insist on paying for meals at times so that they will know that you are not an opportunist. (Note: You do not have to be genuinely insistent. It's a trick to win their regard for you.)
8. Tell them that you love them for who they are and not what they have.

LIVE PERFORMANCES

In case you did not know, singing has health benefits. According to the website of the Barbershop Harmony Society(2020), "singing releases endorphins into your system and makes you feel energized and uplifted. People who sing are healthier than people who don't". Singing for pleasure is not the same as singing on stage before a live audience. Singing on stage before a live audience calls for a great deal of courage and confidence, just like public speaking. Below are some tips for singing gleaned from personal experience and personal conversations.

Tips for Singing

1. Express yourself through your body parts, e.g. your arms, eyes, legs, etc. Showmanship is part of excellent singing.
2. Sing with emotion. Feel the emotion of a song and express the emotion of the song through your vocal prowess and body language.
3. Breathe well and sing from the diaphragm. Excellent singing is a matter of breathing well.
4. Sing with vibrato.
5. Record your singing with a phone/recorder and listen to it to determine those areas that have room for improvement.

6. Enunciate your words. Excellent singing is related to excellent pronunciation.
7. If necessary, sing with falsetto.
8. Have fun singing. This will help you to avoid feeling nervous.
9. Do your best and make progress in your singing as time progresses.
10. Warm up your voice before singing.
11. To hit (extremely) high notes, look up instead of looking down or at the audience.

HOW TO ORGANIZE SCHOOL PARTIES

Ideas for Parties

1. The song "Ha La La La" (http://www.youtube.com/watch?v=v7zh_yCar48)
2. The Chuga Dance (http://www.youtube.com/watch?v=bWus9rLU7c4)
3. Riddles
4. 2 or 3 magic tricks
5. Games – Pass the Parcel, Simon Says, The Human Jackpot, Musical Chairs, etc.
6. The Statue Dance
7. The Newspaper Dance
8. The action song entitled "As We Walk to the Right (A New Friend Found)" (https://www.youtube.com/watch?v=8LgGzmH-a28)
9. The game called "Honey, I Love You, Won't You Give Me A Smile?" (https://www.youtube.com/watch?v=ePuYr52b6yY)
10. A Great Wind Blows (The game could be exciting with hilarious instructions.)
11. A tongue twister competition
12. Two Truths & 1 Lie
13. Chinese whispers
14. On-stage dance lessons (The emcee teaches some dance moves to the selected members of the audience, who copy the steps.)
15. An eating competition
16. A pick-up line/the most romantic proposal contest
17. Limbo Rock
18. The Audience Orchestra (The emcee acts as an orchestra conductor, and the audience is divided into groups with differently assigned sounds. The conductor instructs the

63

different groups to produce the requested sounds by pointing the stick at them to compose a melody spontaneously.)

19. Dance songs, e.g. "Gangnam Style", "Gentleman"(Psy), "The Numa Numa Song" (0-Zone), "Dance Monkey"(Tones & I), "Watch Me"(Silento), "On The Floor"(Jennifer Lopez), "Give Me Everything"(Pitbull), "5, 6, 7, 8"(Steps), "Take You Dancing"(Jason Derulo), "Only Girl (In The World)" (Rihanna), "Uptown Funk"(Bruno Mars), "Roses(Imanbek Remix)"(St Jhn), songs by Vengaboys, Black Eyed Peas, Abba, Boney M, Michael Jackson, etc.

20. A dance competition to select the best Beyonce, Michael Jackson, etc. or a spontaneous TikTok dance challenge

21. A synchronized dance such as the "The Ketchup Song" dance, the "Macarena" dance, the "Nutbush City Limits" dance, etc.

22. A slide show of memorable events

23. A basic salsa dance lesson(The guests take it in turns to dance with various partners.)

24. Charades

25. A traffic light party, i.e. a party where the dress code is either red, yellow or green (red means "taken", yellow means "undecided" and green means "single")

26. An informal singing/karaoke contest with hilarious judges

THE END

REFERENCES

Barbershop Harmony Society.(2019).*The Health Benefits of Singing*. Retrieved November 4, 2020, from https://www.barbershop.org/ the-health-benefits-of-singing

Exploring Your Mind. (2020). *Socrates' Triple Filter Test*. Retrieved November 6, 2020, from https://exploringyourmind.com/ socrates-triple-filter-test/

Shatz, I.(n.d.). *The Humor Effect: On the Benefits of Humor and How to Use it Effectively*. Retrieved November 9, 2020, from https://effectiviology. com/humor-effect/

Skills You Need.(2020).*Interpersonal Skills*. Retrieved November 4, 2020, from https://www.skillsyouneed.com/interpersonal-skills. html#:~:text=Good%20interpersonal%20skills%20help%20 you,before%20they%20become%20big%20issues

Stacey.(2012). *Building Rapport with Humour*. Retrieved November 9, 2020, from https://www.onehourtranslation.com/translation/blog/ building-rapport-humour

10 Amusing Marketing Concepts.(2013). Retrieved November 4, 2020, from https://virtual-kidspace.blogspot.com/2013/06/10-amusing-marketing-concepts.html

The Social Dilemma. Argent Pictures, 2020.*Netflix, https://www.netflix. com/watch/81254224?trackId=13752289&tctx=0%2C0%2C48534f70da 533d0f17b0dec99f60628d391318f2%3A13ae1cda3c1ec04a75a1590b 618265aaf94b372a%2C48534f70da533d0f17b0dec99f60628d391318f 2%3A13ae1cda3c1ec04a75a1590b618265aaf94b372a%2C%2C*

Vital, M.(2014). *9 Types Of Intelligence – Infographic.* Retrieved November 4, 2020, from https://blog.adioma. com/9-types-of-intelligence-infographic/

Youth Employment UK.(2020).*Build Your Self Management Skills.* Retrieved November 4, 2020, from https://www. youthemployment.org.uk/young-professional-training/ self-management-skills-young-professional/

THE FINAL NOTE BY THE AUTHOR

Thank you very much for reading the book. I hope you have benefited from it tremendously and at the same time, enjoyed it immensely. **Please feel free to correspond with the publisher** as I am always eager to seek your feedback, suggestions for further improvement, or recommendations.

Printed in the United States
by Baker & Taylor Publisher Services